First Facts

T0052277

George Washington Carver

BOTANIST AND INVENTOR

by Mary Boone

CAPSTONE PRESS
a capstone imprint

First Facts are published by Capstone Press,
1710 Roe Crest Drive, North Mankato, Minnesota 56003
www.mycapstone.com

Library of Congress Cataloging-in-Publication Data:
Library of Congress Cataloging-in-Publication Data is available on the Library of
Congress website.
ISBN: 978-1-5435-0646-4 (library binding) -- 978-1-5435-0652-5 (paperback) --
978-1-5435-0658-7 (ebook)
Summary: This book presents the life of George Washington Carver, the inventor who
discovered over 300 uses for peanuts.

Editorial Credits
Anna Butzer, editor; Bobbie Nuytten, designer;
Jo Miller, media researcher; Laura Manthe, production specialist

Photo Credits
Getty Images: Anthony Barboza/Contributor, 11, Bettmann/Contributor, 13, 19;
iStockphoto: munst64804, 7; Library of Congress, 14; Newscom: akg-images, 9;
Shutterstock: Everett Historical, cover, (left), Hein Nouwens, cover, (right),
Jeffrey M. Frank, 21; U.S. Department of Agriculture: NARA; Wikimedia:
Adam Cueren, USDA/NARA

Design Elements
Shutterstock: Hein Nouwens

Printed in the United States of America.
010868S18

Table of Contents

CHAPTER 1

Growing Up

Most people look at the peanut and think *snack food.*

George Washington Carver looked further. He used the peanut to make products such as shoe polish and shampoo. His **imagination** helped him develop hundreds of uses for this plant. He became one of the world's most famous inventors.

imagination—the ability to form pictures in your mind of things that are not present or real

George Washington Carver, 1906

George was born around 1864 in Diamond, Missouri. His parents, Mary and Giles, were slaves. When he was just one week old, George, his mother, and his sister were kidnapped. George was soon found and returned to slave owners Moses and Susan Carver. They decided to raise and educate him and his brother, James.

FACT In 1865 the 13th Amendment was added to the U.S. Constitution. It made owning slaves illegal.

George Washington Carver National Monument in Diamond, Missouri

CHAPTER 2

Love of Learning

When George was young, few schools would allow African-American students. Susan Carver taught George at home. George liked learning about plants the most. He loved to care for the Carvers' gardens. He often nursed dying flowers back to health. People called him "The Plant Doctor."

George painting a plant

George moved away from home at age 11. He went to school in Neosho, Missouri. After high school he attended Simpson College. He loved learning about flowers. A teacher suggested he go to Iowa State University to study botany. In 1891 he became the first African-American student at that school. He graduated in 1894.

FACT George Washington Carver was the first African-American to have a national park named after him. The park is near his birthplace in Missouri.

botany—the study of plants

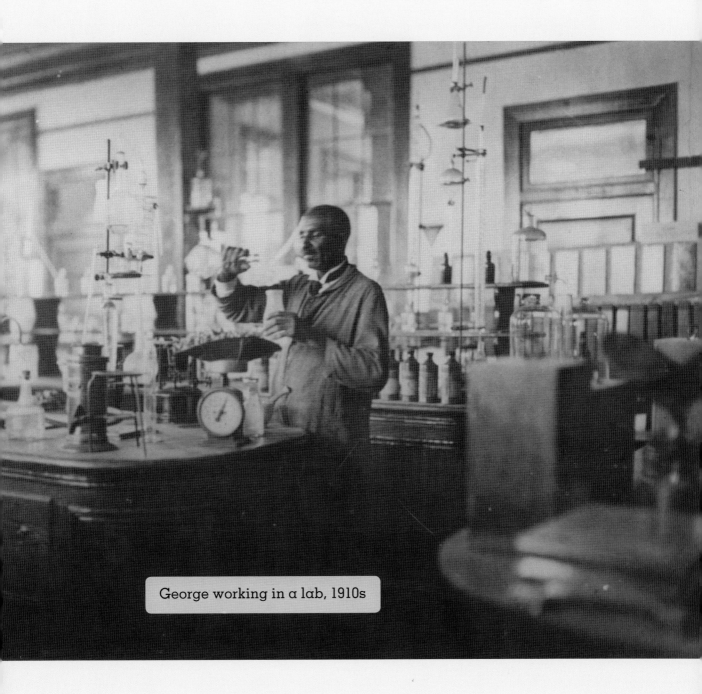

George working in a lab, 1910s

CHAPTER 3

Research and Inventions

George taught at Iowa State University for two years. In 1896 educator Booker T. Washington asked him to take a job at Tuskegee Institute in Alabama. Tuskegee educated African-American students. At the time many other schools would not. George taught **techniques** that could help Southern farmers.

technique—a method or a way of doing something that requires skill

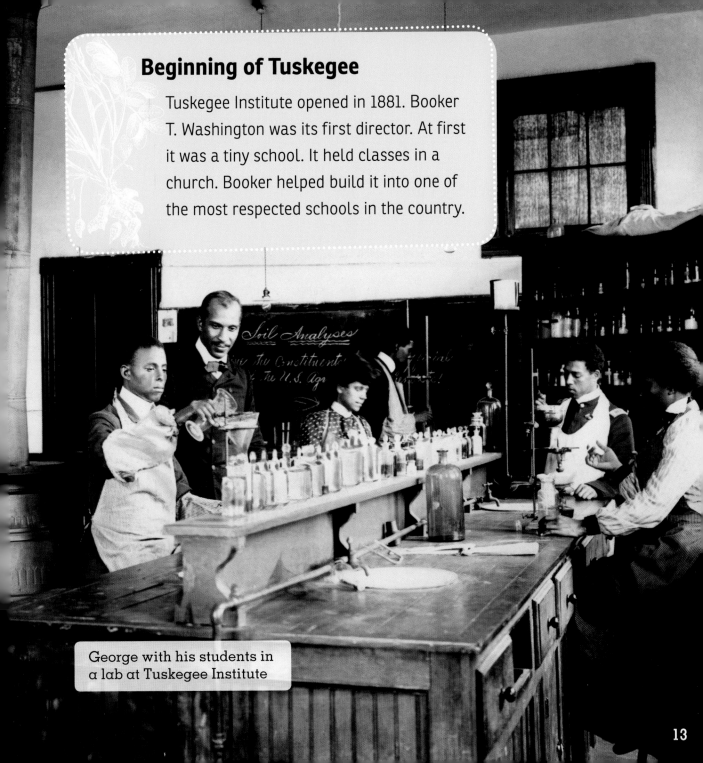

Beginning of Tuskegee

Tuskegee Institute opened in 1881. Booker T. Washington was its first director. At first it was a tiny school. It held classes in a church. Booker helped build it into one of the most respected schools in the country.

George with his students in a lab at Tuskegee Institute

One of George's big ideas was to keep the soil full of **nutrients**. Soil was healthier when farmers planted cotton one year and peanuts the next. This method became known as crop **rotation**. Farmers still use it today.

George looking at soil from a field

nutrient—substances, such as vitamins, that plants and animals need for good health

rotation—regularly changing something by replacing it with something else

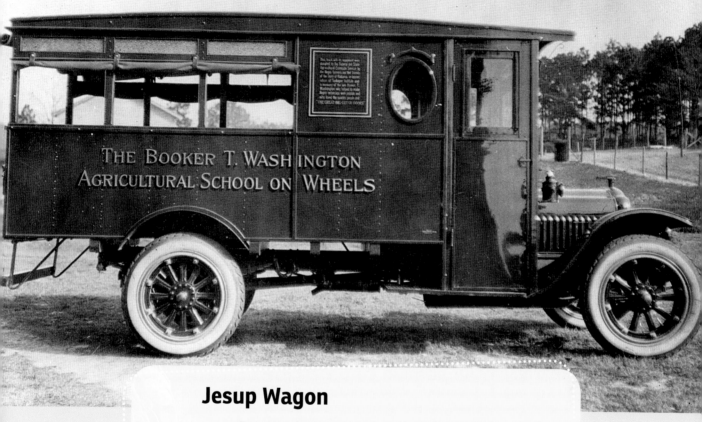

Jesup Wagon

George designed a movable school to take his lessons to the farmers. The first movable school was a horse-drawn cart. He called it a Jesup Wagon. It was named for Morris K. Jesup. Jesup was businessman who helped pay for George's work. Later on, the cart changed to a motorized vehicle.

CHAPTER 4

His Ideas Live On

Rotating crops helped farmers grow more cotton. But now they had a new problem. What could they do with all the peanuts? George helped. He found new things to make with peanuts, such as shaving cream and flour. In total, he came up with more than 300 uses for peanuts.

Service to Others

George got **patents** for only three of his inventions. As a result, he did not make much money. George did not care about being rich. He just wanted to help others.

patent—a legal document giving someone sole rights to make or sell a product

George was respected around the world for his farming knowledge. He gave advice to U.S. Presidents Calvin Coolidge and Franklin D. Roosevelt. Leaders from other countries also asked for his help. They wanted him to show farmers how to improve their soil to help crops grow.

"When you do the common things in life in an uncommon way, you will command the attention of the world."

George Washington Carver

George Washington Carver taught at Tuskegee from 1896 until his death in 1943. He left his entire life savings to the school. The money helped build a new research center. He is buried on the Tuskegee **campus** near Booker T. Washington.

FACT The George W. Carver Museum is located on the Tuskegee campus.

campus—the area and buildings around a university or school

Tuskegee Institute

Glossary

botany (BOT-uh-nee)—the study of plants

campus (KAM-puhss)—the area and buildings around a university or school

imagination (i-maj-uh-NAY-shuhn)—the ability to form pictures in your mind of things that are not present or real

nutrient (NOO-tree-uhnt)—substances, such as vitamins, that plants and animals need for good health

patent (PAT-uhnt)—a legal document giving someone sole rights to make or sell a product

rotation (roh-TAY-shuhn)—regularly changing something by replacing it with something else

technique (tek-NEEK)—a method or a way of doing something that requires skill

Read More

Boyer, Crispin. *Why?: Over 1,111 Answers to Everything.* Washington, D.C.: National Geographic, 2015.

Flynn, Riley. *Booker T. Washington.* Great African Americans. North Mankato, Minn.: Capstone Press, 2014.

Gigliotti, Jim. *Who Was George Washington Carver?.* New York: Grosset & Dunlap, 2015.

Internet Sites

Use Facthound to find Internet sites related to this book.

Visit *www.facthound.com*

Just type in 9781543506464 and go!

Check out projects, games and lots more at
www.capstonekids.com

Critical Thinking Questions

1. George Washington Carver discovered new uses for peanuts. What are some of the things you use today as a result of George's discoveries?

2. George designed a movable school to help farmers far away. Do you think something like that would be useful today? Why or why not?

3. Using online sources, find out what ideas George Washington Carver had for using peanuts. Which ones do you think would have worked the best? Why?

Index